TULSA CITY-COUNTY LIBRARY

BACKYARD ANIMALS

WOLF

Katie Gillespie

AV2
www.av2books.com

Step 1
Go to **www.av2books.com**

Step 2
Enter this unique code

QZMOEOZ7L

Step 3
Explore your interactive eBook!

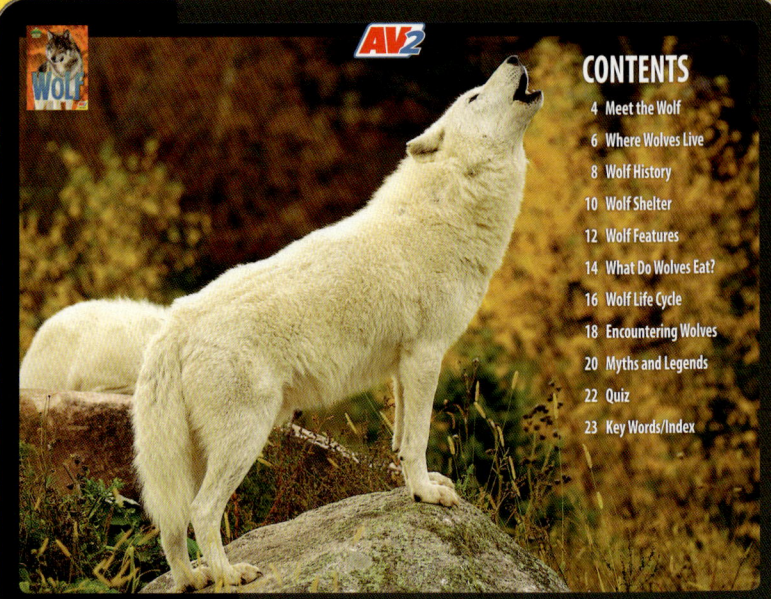

AV2 is optimized for use on any device

Your interactive eBook comes with...

Contents
Browse a live contents page to easily navigate through resources

Audio
Listen to sections of the book read aloud

Videos
Watch informative video clips

Weblinks
Gain additional information for research

Try This!
Complete activities and hands-on experiments

Key Words
Study vocabulary, and complete a matching word activity

Quizzes
Test your knowledge

Slideshows
View images and captions

... and much, much more!

View new titles and product videos at www.av2books.com

Contents

AV2 Book Code	2
Meet the Wolf	4
Where Wolves Live	6
Wolf History	8
Wolf Shelter	10
Wolf Features	12
What Do Wolves Eat?	14
Wolf Life Cycle	16
Encountering Wolves	18
Myths and Legends	20
Quiz	22
Key Words/Index	23

Meet the Wolf

Wolves are **mammals**. They are large, doglike animals that move around in **packs**. They are powerful hunters and fast runners.

Wolves are known for their loud, long howl. A lone wolf may howl for many different reasons. Sometimes, a wolf howls to get in touch with its pack during a hunt. Other times, it howls because of an emergency, or to **communicate** across large distances. An individual wolf's howl is unique, like a human fingerprint.

A wolf's howl can carry **6 miles** (10 kilometers) through the forest, and **10 miles** (16 km) across tundra.

Where Wolves Live

The wolf is from the same family as the dog. They are both **canines**. There are different **species** of wolf all over the world. Wolves can be found in China, Russia, Europe, Canada, and the United States.

Wolves mostly live in cold climates, where there are few people. Some wolves live in warmer climates, such as Greece or India. Rare species of wolf can only be found in certain parts of the world. For instance, the Abyssinian wolf only lives in the mountain regions of Ethiopia in Africa.

Gray wolves are the most common type of wolf on Earth.

Backyard Animals

Wolf History

Wolves' closest relatives were small, **carnivorous** mammals known as *miacids*. They had long hind legs and a doglike **pelvis**. Miacids first lived about 60 million years ago.

Between 30 and 40 million years ago, the miacid became a creature known as *Cynodictis*. It was the first true dog. Over time, this small animal's family tree split into two branches. The branch known as *Tomarctus* is an **ancestor** of the wolves we know today.

Some scientists think that the **first** gray wolf came to North America about **500,000 years** ago.

Backyard Animals

Dire wolves once lived in North America, between 11,700 and 2.6 million years ago. These fierce animals were larger and more powerful than modern wolves.

Wolf 9

Wolf Shelter

Wolves take shelter in places called dens. Dens can be made in between large rocks, inside a hollow log, or under the overhang of a cliff. Wolves may use the same den for many years.

The area that a wolf lives in is called its **territory**. This territory can be as large as 70 square miles (181 square km). Wolves have many rules about how each pack controls its own territory. Packs will fight other wolves and other animals to maintain their space.

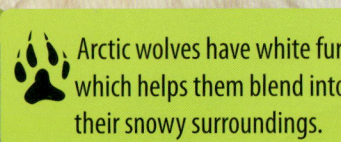
Arctic wolves have white fur, which helps them blend into their snowy surroundings.

Backyard Animals

Wolves like to live near water and places where they can find food easily.

Wolf 11

Wolf Features

Wolves are some of the best **predators** in the animal kingdom. They have many features that help them run fast and find **prey**. Wolves are expertly equipped to survive in nature.

FUR
Wolves have thick fur. The outer layer of fur is made of long, coarse hair. The inner layer is thick and fluffy.

LEGS AND PAWS
Wolves have powerful legs. Their large, broad paws help them move across snow and soft ground without sinking. Wolves can run for 22 miles (35 km) without stopping.

EARS
Wolves have large, pointed ears. Their sense of hearing is very good. Wolves can pick up sounds more than 6 miles (10 km) away.

NOSE
Wolves have a strong sense of smell. They use it as a tool to find food. They can smell animals that are more than 1 mile (1.6 km) away.

MOUTH
A wolf's jaws are twice as strong as a German Shepherd's. Wolves have very sharp teeth to help them tear meat from their prey. This also makes it easy for them to carry prey long distances to the rest of the pack.

Wolf

What Do Wolves Eat?

A wolf's diet is made up mainly of meat. However, wolves can also eat grass and berries. Depending on where they live, wolves hunt different types of prey.

Often, the prey that wolves hunt is much bigger than the wolves themselves. To help with this, wolves hunt in packs. This lets them take down larger animals. Wolves also make sure to hunt weaker targets. Small or sick animals are easier to catch.

A wolf can eat almost 20 percent of its body weight in one meal.

Backyard Animals

An elk can weigh almost six times as much as a wolf. This does not stop a wolf pack from bringing one down.

Wolf 15

Wolf Life Cycle

Only the strongest male and female in a pack will breed. They are known as the alpha male and the alpha female. The males in the pack fight each other to find out who is the strongest. The most powerful male becomes the alpha male.

Birth to 2 Months Old
Wolf pups spend their first two months sleeping and feeding on their mother's milk. They can barely open their eyes. Their sense of smell is weak.

2 Years and Older
The pups are considered adults when they are about 2 years old. Once a wolf reaches this age, it can start to mate. Male and female wolves usually mate for life. Wolves live for about 7 to 10 years.

The female digs a den where she will give birth to her babies, or pups. She can give birth to between 3 and 14 pups in one litter. The entire wolf pack helps to raise the pups.

3 Months Old

At 3 months old, the pups slowly meet the rest of the pack. They begin play-fighting with other pups. Their fur starts to grow. The pups are able to eat the same meat as the adults.

9 Months Old

By 9 months old, the pups have their full coat of fur. They start to hunt for their own meat. Their teeth begin to get sharper. Now, the pups are almost the same size as the adults.

Encountering Wolves

Wolves do not often live in places where there are many humans. Unlike other animals, wolves do not run away when they see humans. Instead, they become alert. They may even attack if they sense any danger.

People may see wolves when they are exploring in nature. At times, people may even come across an entire pack of wolves. If you see a wolf, it is best to keep your distance. Make loud noises to scare the animal away. Try to walk to a safe place.

Wolves usually live in packs of about 6 to 10.

People should never approach an adult wolf or a wolf pup.

Wolf 19

Myths and Legends

There are many stories in which wolves are seen as dangerous and wicked. Children's tales often have a mean wolf character. In these stories, wolves are greedy and evil animals. For instance, the wolf in *Little Red Riding Hood* tries to eat the girl and her grandmother.

However, some stories show how wolves can be good examples. The mother wolf in *The Jungle Book* is a positive character. She looks after Mowgli, a human child, along with her cubs.

After the Big Bad Wolf meets Little Red Riding Hood in the woods, he tries to trick her by pretending to be her grandmother.

The Myth of Romulus and Remus

Romulus and Remus were twin brothers. When they were babies, their parents put them in a basket on the Tiber River. The basket slowly drifted onto the riverbank, where the twins were discovered by a female wolf. The wolf cared for the babies until a shepherd found them. The shepherd raised the twins.

When Romulus and Remus grew up, they decided to build a city where the wolf had found them. Once they had built the city, the brothers argued about what it should be called. They both wanted to name it after themselves. In the end, Romulus won the fight. He became the king of the new city and named it "Rome" in his honor. This is how the city of Rome was founded.

Quiz

1 What type of animal is a wolf?

2 What is the most common type of wolf?

3 How long do wolves usually live?

4 What makes up the main part of a wolf's diet?

5 What kind of climate do most wolves live in?

6 How many pups can a female wolf give birth to in one litter?

7 What is the area that a wolf lives in called?

8 How far can wolves run without stopping?

ANSWERS:
1. Mammal 2. Gray wolf 3. About 7 to 10 years 4. Meat 5. A cold climate 6. Between 3 and 14 7. Its territory 8. 22 miles (35 km)

Backyard Animals

Key Words

ancestor: a relative who lived a long time ago

canines: a family of mammals that include the dog and the fox

carnivorous: feeding on other animals

communicate: to make sounds in order to share information

mammals: warm-blooded, live-born animals that have a spine, fur or hair, and drink milk from their mother

packs: groups of wolves

pelvis: the bony structure near the base of the spine where the legs are attached

predators: animals that hunt other animals

prey: an animal that is hunted for food

species: animals or plants that share certain features and can breed together

territory: the land on which a pack of wolves lives and hunts

Index

Abyssinian wolf 6

canines 6

dens 10, 17
dire wolves 9

fur 10, 12, 17

gray wolf 6, 7, 8, 22

howl 4, 5

life cycle 16, 17

packs 4, 10, 13, 14, 15, 16, 17, 18
prey 11, 12, 13, 14
pups 16, 17, 19, 22

red wolf 7

Get the best of both worlds.

AV2 bridges the gap between print and digital.

The expandable resources toolbar enables quick access to content including **videos**, **audio**, **activities**, **weblinks**, **slideshows**, **quizzes**, and **key words**.

Animated videos make static images come alive.

Resource icons on each page help readers to further **explore key concepts**.

Published by AV2
350 5th Avenue, 59th Floor
New York, NY 10118
Website: www.av2books.com

Copyright © 2021 AV2
All rights reserved. No part of this publication may be reproduced, stored in a retrieval system, or transmitted in any form or by any means, electronic, mechanical, photocopying, recording, or otherwise, without the prior written permission of the publisher.

Library of Congress Control Number: 2019955087
ISBN 978-1-7911-2075-7 (hardcover)
ISBN 978-1-7911-2076-4 (softcover)
ISBN 978-1-7911-2077-1 (multi-user eBook)
ISBN 978-1-7911-2078-8 (single-user eBook)

Printed in Guangzhou, China
1 2 3 4 5 6 7 8 9 0 24 23 22 21 20

022020
101119

Editor: Katie Gillespie
Designer: Ana María Vidal

Every reasonable effort has been made to trace ownership and to obtain permission to reprint copyright material. The publishers would be pleased to have any errors or omissions brought to their attention so that they may be corrected in subsequent printings.

AV2 acknowledges Getty Images, Alamy, Minden Pictures, iStock, and Shutterstock as its primary image suppliers for this title.

View new titles and product videos at www.av2books.com